This Pet Journal Belongs To:

_____

MY PET Profile

NAME:

BREED:

BIRTHDAY:

GENDER:

ID CHIP #:

ALLERGIES:

COAT COLOR:

EYE COLOR:

SPECIAL MARKINGS:

MEDICAL CONDITIONS:

WEIGHT :

FAVORITE TOYS:

SPAY/NEUTERED:	YES:	NO:
NOTES:		

Vet Information

NAME/BUSINESS:

PHONE:

EMAIL:

ADDRESS:

Groomer Information

NAME/BUSINESS:

PHONE:

EMAIL:

ADDRESS:

VETERINARY CARE *Tracker*

DATE:	DESCRIPTION:	LOCATION:	AMOUNT:

PET HEALTH
Immunization Records

DATE:	AGE:	TYPE:	GIVEN BY:	NEXT DUE:

PET HEALTH
Medication Records

DATE:	AGE:	MEDICATION:	GIVEN BY:	NEXT DUE:

PET MEDICATION *Tracker*

DATE & TIME:	MEDICATION:	FREQUENCY:	DOSAGE:

PET SITTER *Notes*

- RESPONSIBILITIES -

	M	T	W	T	F	S	S

WEEKLY PET *Journal*

WEEK OF: ....

MONDAY	TUESDAY	WEDNESDAY

THURSDAY	FRIDAY	SATURDAY

SUNDAY	WEEKLY NOTES

DAILY PET *Journal*

DAILY MEALS

APPETITE:	GOOD	FAIR	POOR
MORNING:			
AFTERNOON:			
EVENING:			

FOOD PROVIDED

TREATS

MOOD

PLAY TIME

NOTES

SLEEP TIMES:

ACTIVITIES:	INDOORS	OUTDOORS

NOTES

DAILY PET *Journal*

DAILY MEALS

APPETITE:	GOOD	FAIR	POOR
MORNING:			
AFTERNOON:			
EVENING:			

FOOD PROVIDED

TREATS

MOOD

PLAY TIME

NOTES

SLEEP TIMES:

ACTIVITIES:

	INDOORS	OUTDOORS

NOTES

DAILY PET *Journal*

DAILY MEALS

APPETITE:	GOOD	FAIR	POOR
MORNING:			
AFTERNOON:			
EVENING:			

FOOD PROVIDED

TREATS

MOOD

PLAY TIME

NOTES

SLEEP TIMES:

ACTIVITIES:	INDOORS	OUTDOORS

NOTES

DAILY PET *Journal*

DAILY MEALS

APPETITE:	GOOD	FAIR	POOR
MORNING:			
AFTERNOON:			
EVENING:			

FOOD PROVIDED

TREATS

MOOD

PLAY TIME

NOTES

SLEEP TIMES:

ACTIVITIES:

	INDOORS	OUTDOORS

NOTES

DAILY PET *Journal*

DAILY MEALS

APPETITE:	GOOD	FAIR	POOR
MORNING:			
AFTERNOON:			
EVENING:			

FOOD PROVIDED

TREATS

MOOD

PLAY TIME

NOTES

SLEEP TIMES:

ACTIVITIES:	INDOORS	OUTDOORS

NOTES

DAILY PET *Journal*

DAILY MEALS

APPETITE:	GOOD	FAIR	POOR
MORNING:			
AFTERNOON:			
EVENING:			

FOOD PROVIDED

TREATS

MOOD

PLAY TIME

NOTES

SLEEP TIMES:

ACTIVITIES:	INDOORS	OUTDOORS

NOTES

DAILY PET *Journal*

DAILY MEALS

APPETITE:	GOOD	FAIR	POOR
MORNING:			
AFTERNOON:			
EVENING:			

FOOD PROVIDED

TREATS

MOOD

PLAY TIME

NOTES

SLEEP TIMES:

ACTIVITIES:	INDOORS	OUTDOORS

NOTES

MY PET Expenses

MONTH: **YEAR:**

PET NAME:

EXPENSE TRACKER

DATE	FOOD	VET	MEDICATION	GROOMING	COST
					$
					$
					$
					$
					$
					$
					$
					$
					$
					$
					$
					$
					$
					$
					$
					$
					$
					$

PET Vaccination Chart

YEAR: _____

PET NAME:	DOB:	GENDER:

VACCINATION HISTORY

DATE:	VACCINATION:	AGE:	NOTES:

PET WELLNESS Journal

YEAR: _____

PET NAME:		DOB:	GENDER:

WELLNESS HISTORY

DATE:	DESCRIPTION:	TREATMENT:	NOTES:

MONTHLY PET *Journal*

JANUARY

FEBRUARY

MARCH

APRIL

MAY

JUNE

MONTHLY PET *Journal*

JULY

AUGUST

SEPTEMBER

OCTOBER

NOVEMBER

DECEMBER

MY PET Journal

MY PET Journal

MY PET *Journal*

WEEKLY PET *Journal*

WEEK OF: ....

MONDAY	TUESDAY	WEDNESDAY

THURSDAY	FRIDAY	SATURDAY

SUNDAY	WEEKLY NOTES

DAILY PET *Journal*

DAILY MEALS

APPETITE:	GOOD	FAIR	POOR
MORNING:			
AFTERNOON:			
EVENING:			

FOOD PROVIDED

TREATS

MOOD

PLAY TIME

NOTES

SLEEP TIMES:

ACTIVITIES:	INDOORS	OUTDOORS

NOTES

DAILY PET *Journal*

DAILY MEALS

APPETITE:	GOOD	FAIR	POOR
MORNING:			
AFTERNOON:			
EVENING:			

FOOD PROVIDED

TREATS

MOOD

PLAY TIME

NOTES

SLEEP TIMES:

ACTIVITIES:

	INDOORS	OUTDOORS

NOTES

DAILY PET *Journal*

DAILY MEALS

APPETITE:	GOOD	FAIR	POOR
MORNING:			
AFTERNOON:			
EVENING:			

FOOD PROVIDED

TREATS

MOOD

PLAY TIME

NOTES

SLEEP TIMES:

ACTIVITIES:	INDOORS	OUTDOORS

NOTES

DAILY PET *Journal*

DAILY MEALS

APPETITE:	GOOD	FAIR	POOR
MORNING:			
AFTERNOON:			
EVENING:			

FOOD PROVIDED

TREATS

MOOD

PLAY TIME

NOTES

SLEEP TIMES:

ACTIVITIES:

	INDOORS	OUTDOORS

NOTES

DAILY PET *Journal*

DAILY MEALS

APPETITE:	GOOD	FAIR	POOR
MORNING:			
AFTERNOON:			
EVENING:			

FOOD PROVIDED

TREATS

MOOD

PLAY TIME

NOTES

SLEEP TIMES:

ACTIVITIES:	INDOORS	OUTDOORS

NOTES

DAILY PET *Journal*

DAILY MEALS

APPETITE:	GOOD	FAIR	POOR
MORNING:			
AFTERNOON:			
EVENING:			

FOOD PROVIDED

TREATS

MOOD

PLAY TIME

NOTES

SLEEP TIMES:

ACTIVITIES:

	INDOORS	OUTDOORS

NOTES

DAILY PET *Journal*

DAILY MEALS

APPETITE:	GOOD	FAIR	POOR
MORNING:			
AFTERNOON:			
EVENING:			

FOOD PROVIDED

TREATS

MOOD

PLAY TIME

NOTES

SLEEP TIMES:

ACTIVITIES:		INDOORS	OUTDOORS

NOTES

MY PET Expenses

MONTH: _____   **YEAR:** _____

PET NAME: _____

EXPENSE TRACKER

DATE	FOOD	VET	MEDICATION	GROOMING	COST
					$
					$
					$
					$
					$
					$
					$
					$
					$
					$
					$
					$
					$
					$
					$
					$
					$

PET Vaccination Chart

YEAR:

PET NAME:	DOB:	GENDER:

VACCINATION HISTORY

DATE:	VACCINATION:	AGE:	NOTES:

PET WELLNESS *Journal*

YEAR:

PET NAME:	DOB:	GENDER:

WELLNESS HISTORY

DATE:	DESCRIPTION:	TREATMENT:	NOTES:

MY PET Journal

_____

_____

_____

_____

_____

_____

_____

_____

_____

_____

_____

_____

_____

_____

_____

_____

_____

_____

MY PET *Journal*

_____
_____
_____
_____
_____
_____
_____
_____
_____
_____
_____
_____
_____
_____
_____
_____
_____
_____
_____
_____

MY PET Journal

_____
_____
_____
_____
_____
_____
_____
_____
_____
_____
_____
_____
_____
_____
_____
_____
_____
_____

WEEKLY PET *Journal*

WEEK OF: ....

MONDAY

TUESDAY

WEDNESDAY

THURSDAY

FRIDAY

SATURDAY

SUNDAY

WEEKLY NOTES

DAILY PET Journal

DAILY MEALS

APPETITE:	GOOD	FAIR	POOR
MORNING:			
AFTERNOON:			
EVENING:			

FOOD PROVIDED

TREATS

PLAY TIME

MOOD

NOTES

SLEEP TIMES:

ACTIVITIES:	INDOORS	OUTDOORS

NOTES

DAILY PET *Journal*

DAILY MEALS

APPETITE:	GOOD	FAIR	POOR
MORNING:			
AFTERNOON:			
EVENING:			

FOOD PROVIDED

TREATS

MOOD

PLAY TIME

NOTES

SLEEP TIMES:

ACTIVITIES:

	INDOORS	OUTDOORS

NOTES

DAILY PET Journal

DAILY MEALS

APPETITE:	GOOD	FAIR	POOR
MORNING:			
AFTERNOON:			
EVENING:			

FOOD PROVIDED

TREATS

MOOD

PLAY TIME

NOTES

SLEEP TIMES:

ACTIVITIES:

	INDOORS	OUTDOORS

NOTES

DAILY PET *Journal*

DAILY MEALS

APPETITE:	GOOD	FAIR	POOR
MORNING:			
AFTERNOON:			
EVENING:			

FOOD PROVIDED

TREATS

MOOD

PLAY TIME

NOTES

SLEEP TIMES:

ACTIVITIES:	INDOORS	OUTDOORS

NOTES

DAILY PET Journal

DAILY MEALS

APPETITE:	GOOD	FAIR	POOR
MORNING:			
AFTERNOON:			
EVENING:			

FOOD PROVIDED

TREATS

MOOD

PLAY TIME

NOTES

SLEEP TIMES:

ACTIVITIES:	INDOORS	OUTDOORS

NOTES

DAILY PET Journal

DAILY MEALS

APPETITE:	GOOD	FAIR	POOR
MORNING:			
AFTERNOON:			
EVENING:			

FOOD PROVIDED

TREATS

MOOD

PLAY TIME

NOTES

SLEEP TIMES:

ACTIVITIES:	INDOORS	OUTDOORS

NOTES

DAILY PET *Journal*

DAILY MEALS

APPETITE:	GOOD	FAIR	POOR
MORNING:			
AFTERNOON:			
EVENING:			

FOOD PROVIDED

TREATS

PLAY TIME

MOOD

NOTES

SLEEP TIMES:

ACTIVITIES:	INDOORS	OUTDOORS

NOTES

MY PET Expenses

MONTH: _____   **YEAR:** _____

PET NAME: _____

EXPENSE TRACKER

DATE	FOOD	VET	MEDICATION	GROOMING	COST
					$
					$
					$
					$
					$
					$
					$
					$
					$
					$
					$
					$
					$
					$
					$
					$

PET Vaccination Chart

YEAR: _____

PET NAME:	DOB:	GENDER:

VACCINATION HISTORY

DATE:	VACCINATION:	AGE:	NOTES:

PET WELLNESS Journal

YEAR: _____

PET NAME:	DOB:	GENDER:

WELLNESS HISTORY

DATE:	DESCRIPTION:	TREATMENT:	NOTES:

MY PET Journal

MY PET Journal

MY PET Journal

_____
_____
_____
_____
_____
_____
_____
_____
_____
_____
_____
_____
_____
_____
_____
_____
_____
_____
_____
_____

WEEKLY PET *Journal*

WEEK OF: ....

MONDAY	TUESDAY	WEDNESDAY

THURSDAY	FRIDAY	SATURDAY

SUNDAY	WEEKLY NOTES

DAILY PET *Journal*

DAILY MEALS

APPETITE:	GOOD	FAIR	POOR
MORNING:			
AFTERNOON:			
EVENING:			

FOOD PROVIDED

TREATS

MOOD

PLAY TIME

NOTES

SLEEP TIMES:

ACTIVITIES:	INDOORS	OUTDOORS

NOTES

DAILY PET *Journal*

DAILY MEALS

APPETITE:	GOOD	FAIR	POOR
MORNING:			
AFTERNOON:			
EVENING:			

FOOD PROVIDED

TREATS

MOOD

PLAY TIME

NOTES

SLEEP TIMES:

ACTIVITIES:	INDOORS	OUTDOORS

NOTES

DAILY PET *Journal*

DAILY MEALS

APPETITE:	GOOD	FAIR	POOR
MORNING:			
AFTERNOON:			
EVENING:			

FOOD PROVIDED

TREATS

PLAY TIME

MOOD

NOTES

SLEEP TIMES:

ACTIVITIES:

	INDOORS	OUTDOORS

NOTES

DAILY PET *Journal*

DAILY MEALS

APPETITE:	GOOD	FAIR	POOR
MORNING:			
AFTERNOON:			
EVENING:			

FOOD PROVIDED

TREATS

MOOD

PLAY TIME

NOTES

SLEEP TIMES:

ACTIVITIES:

	INDOORS	OUTDOORS

NOTES

DAILY PET *Journal*

DAILY MEALS

APPETITE:	GOOD	FAIR	POOR
MORNING:			
AFTERNOON:			
EVENING:			

FOOD PROVIDED

TREATS

MOOD

PLAY TIME

NOTES

SLEEP TIMES:

ACTIVITIES:	INDOORS	OUTDOORS

NOTES

DAILY PET *Journal*

DAILY MEALS

APPETITE:	GOOD	FAIR	POOR
MORNING:			
AFTERNOON:			
EVENING:			

FOOD PROVIDED

TREATS

MOOD

PLAY TIME

NOTES

SLEEP TIMES:

ACTIVITIES:	INDOORS	OUTDOORS

NOTES

DAILY PET *Journal*

DAILY MEALS

APPETITE:	GOOD	FAIR	POOR
MORNING:			
AFTERNOON:			
EVENING:			

FOOD PROVIDED

TREATS

MOOD

PLAY TIME

NOTES

SLEEP TIMES:

ACTIVITIES:	INDOORS	OUTDOORS

NOTES

MY PET Expenses

MONTH: **YEAR:**

PET NAME:

EXPENSE TRACKER

DATE	FOOD	VET	MEDICATION	GROOMING	COST
					$
					$
					$
					$
					$
					$
					$
					$
					$
					$
					$
					$
					$
					$
					$
					$
					$
					$

PET Vaccination Chart

YEAR: _____

PET NAME:		DOB:	GENDER:

VACCINATION HISTORY

DATE:	VACCINATION:	AGE:	NOTES:

PET WELLNESS *Journal*

YEAR:

PET NAME:	DOB:	GENDER:

WELLNESS HISTORY

DATE:	DESCRIPTION:	TREATMENT:	NOTES:

MY PET Journal

MY PET Journal

MY PET Journal

WEEKLY PET *Journal*

WEEK OF: ....

MONDAY	TUESDAY	WEDNESDAY

THURSDAY	FRIDAY	SATURDAY

SUNDAY	WEEKLY NOTES

DAILY PET *Journal*

DAILY MEALS

APPETITE:	GOOD	FAIR	POOR
MORNING:			
AFTERNOON:			
EVENING:			

FOOD PROVIDED

TREATS

MOOD

PLAY TIME

NOTES

SLEEP TIMES:

ACTIVITIES:	INDOORS	OUTDOORS

NOTES

DAILY PET *Journal*

DAILY MEALS

APPETITE:	GOOD	FAIR	POOR
MORNING:			
AFTERNOON:			
EVENING:			

FOOD PROVIDED

TREATS

MOOD

PLAY TIME

NOTES

SLEEP TIMES:

ACTIVITIES:

	INDOORS	OUTDOORS

NOTES

DAILY PET Journal

DAILY MEALS

APPETITE:	GOOD	FAIR	POOR
MORNING:			
AFTERNOON:			
EVENING:			

FOOD PROVIDED

TREATS

MOOD

PLAY TIME

NOTES

SLEEP TIMES:

ACTIVITIES:	INDOORS	OUTDOORS

NOTES

DAILY PET *Journal*

DAILY MEALS

APPETITE:	GOOD	FAIR	POOR
MORNING:			
AFTERNOON:			
EVENING:			

FOOD PROVIDED

TREATS

MOOD

PLAY TIME

NOTES

SLEEP TIMES:

ACTIVITIES:	INDOORS	OUTDOORS

NOTES

DAILY PET *Journal*

DAILY MEALS

APPETITE:	GOOD	FAIR	POOR
MORNING:			
AFTERNOON:			
EVENING:			

FOOD PROVIDED

TREATS

MOOD

PLAY TIME

NOTES

SLEEP TIMES:

ACTIVITIES:	INDOORS	OUTDOORS

NOTES

DAILY PET *Journal*

DAILY MEALS

APPETITE:	GOOD	FAIR	POOR
MORNING:			
AFTERNOON:			
EVENING:			

FOOD PROVIDED

TREATS

MOOD

PLAY TIME

NOTES

SLEEP TIMES:

ACTIVITIES:

	INDOORS	OUTDOORS

NOTES

DAILY PET *Journal*

DAILY MEALS

APPETITE:	GOOD	FAIR	POOR
MORNING:			
AFTERNOON:			
EVENING:			

FOOD PROVIDED

TREATS

PLAY TIME

MOOD

NOTES

SLEEP TIMES:

ACTIVITIES:

	INDOORS	OUTDOORS

NOTES

MY PET Expenses

MONTH: _____ **YEAR:** _____

PET NAME: _____

EXPENSE TRACKER

DATE	FOOD	VET	MEDICATION	GROOMING	COST
					$
					$
					$
					$
					$
					$
					$
					$
					$
					$
					$
					$
					$
					$
					$
					$
					$

PET Vaccination Chart

YEAR: _____

PET NAME:	DOB:	GENDER:

VACCINATION HISTORY

DATE:	VACCINATION:	AGE:	NOTES:

PET WELLNESS Journal

YEAR:

PET NAME:	DOB:	GENDER:

WELLNESS HISTORY

DATE:	DESCRIPTION:	TREATMENT:	NOTES:

MY PET Journal

MY PET Journal

MY PET Journal

WEEKLY PET *Journal*

WEEK OF: ....

MONDAY

TUESDAY

WEDNESDAY

THURSDAY

FRIDAY

SATURDAY

SUNDAY

WEEKLY NOTES

DAILY PET *Journal*

DAILY MEALS

APPETITE:	GOOD	FAIR	POOR
MORNING:			
AFTERNOON:			
EVENING:			

FOOD PROVIDED

TREATS

MOOD

PLAY TIME

NOTES

SLEEP TIMES:

ACTIVITIES:

	INDOORS	OUTDOORS

NOTES

DAILY PET *Journal*

DAILY MEALS

APPETITE:	GOOD	FAIR	POOR
MORNING:			
AFTERNOON:			
EVENING:			

FOOD PROVIDED

TREATS

MOOD

PLAY TIME

NOTES

SLEEP TIMES:

ACTIVITIES:	INDOORS	OUTDOORS

NOTES

DAILY PET *Journal*

DAILY MEALS

APPETITE:	GOOD	FAIR	POOR
MORNING:			
AFTERNOON:			
EVENING:			

FOOD PROVIDED

TREATS

MOOD

PLAY TIME

NOTES

SLEEP TIMES:

ACTIVITIES:	INDOORS	OUTDOORS

NOTES

DAILY PET *Journal*

DAILY MEALS

APPETITE:	GOOD	FAIR	POOR
MORNING:			
AFTERNOON:			
EVENING:			

FOOD PROVIDED

TREATS

MOOD

PLAY TIME

NOTES

SLEEP TIMES:

ACTIVITIES:	INDOORS	OUTDOORS

NOTES

DAILY PET *Journal*

DAILY MEALS

APPETITE:	GOOD	FAIR	POOR
MORNING:			
AFTERNOON:			
EVENING:			

FOOD PROVIDED

TREATS

MOOD

PLAY TIME

NOTES

SLEEP TIMES:

ACTIVITIES:	INDOORS	OUTDOORS

NOTES

DAILY PET *Journal*

DAILY MEALS

APPETITE:	GOOD	FAIR	POOR
MORNING:			
AFTERNOON:			
EVENING:			

FOOD PROVIDED

TREATS

MOOD

PLAY TIME

NOTES

SLEEP TIMES:

ACTIVITIES:

	INDOORS	OUTDOORS

NOTES

DAILY PET *Journal*

DAILY MEALS

APPETITE:	GOOD	FAIR	POOR
MORNING:			
AFTERNOON:			
EVENING:			

FOOD PROVIDED

TREATS

MOOD

PLAY TIME

NOTES

SLEEP TIMES:

ACTIVITIES:	INDOORS	OUTDOORS

NOTES

MY PET Expenses

MONTH: _____   **YEAR:** _____

PET NAME: _____

EXPENSE TRACKER

DATE	FOOD	VET	MEDICATION	GROOMING	COST
					$
					$
					$
					$
					$
					$
					$
					$
					$
					$
					$
					$
					$
					$
					$
					$
					$

PET Vaccination Chart

YEAR: _____

PET NAME:		DOB:	GENDER:

VACCINATION HISTORY

DATE:	VACCINATION:	AGE:	NOTES:

PET WELLNESS *Journal*

YEAR: _____

PET NAME:	DOB:	GENDER:

WELLNESS HISTORY

DATE:	DESCRIPTION:	TREATMENT:	NOTES:

MY PET Journal

_____
_____
_____
_____
_____
_____
_____
_____
_____
_____
_____
_____
_____
_____
_____
_____

MY PET Journal

MY PET Journal

_____

_____

_____

_____

_____

_____

_____

_____

_____

_____

_____

_____

_____

_____

_____

_____

WEEKLY PET *Journal*

WEEK OF: ....

MONDAY

TUESDAY

WEDNESDAY

THURSDAY

FRIDAY

SATURDAY

SUNDAY

WEEKLY NOTES

DAILY PET *Journal*

DAILY MEALS

APPETITE:	GOOD	FAIR	POOR
MORNING:			
AFTERNOON:			
EVENING:			

FOOD PROVIDED

TREATS

PLAY TIME

MOOD

NOTES

SLEEP TIMES:

ACTIVITIES:	INDOORS	OUTDOORS

NOTES

DAILY PET Journal

DAILY MEALS

APPETITE:	GOOD	FAIR	POOR
MORNING:			
AFTERNOON:			
EVENING:			

FOOD PROVIDED

TREATS

MOOD

PLAY TIME

NOTES

SLEEP TIMES:

ACTIVITIES:	INDOORS	OUTDOORS

NOTES

DAILY PET *Journal*

DAILY MEALS

APPETITE:	GOOD	FAIR	POOR
MORNING:			
AFTERNOON:			
EVENING:			

FOOD PROVIDED

TREATS

MOOD

PLAY TIME

NOTES

SLEEP TIMES:

ACTIVITIES:	INDOORS	OUTDOORS

NOTES

DAILY PET *Journal*

DAILY MEALS

APPETITE:	GOOD	FAIR	POOR
MORNING:			
AFTERNOON:			
EVENING:			

FOOD PROVIDED

TREATS

MOOD

PLAY TIME

NOTES

SLEEP TIMES:

ACTIVITIES:	INDOORS	OUTDOORS

NOTES

DAILY PET *Journal*

DAILY MEALS

APPETITE:	GOOD	FAIR	POOR
MORNING:			
AFTERNOON:			
EVENING:			

FOOD PROVIDED

TREATS

MOOD

PLAY TIME

NOTES

SLEEP TIMES:

ACTIVITIES:

	INDOORS	OUTDOORS

NOTES

Manufactured by Amazon.ca
Bolton, ON